B/W
3-00

CW00732514

Great Railway Eras

CLAPHAM JUNCTION

50 years of change

Vic Mitchell and Keith Smith

MP Middleton Press

Cover pictures: Class U 2-6-0 no. 31624 creeps between platforms 2 and 3 with mixed freight, while a van train is shunted on 9th August 1961. In contrast, an all electric scene was recorded on 12th November 1985 from platform 14, with no. 73134 centre stage while working the 12.15 Victoria to Gatwick Airport express. (Both J.Scrace)

This book commemorates the 50th anniversary of the formation of British Railways upon Nationalisation on 1st January 1948.

Published January 1998

ISBN 1 901706 06 0

© Middleton Press

Design Deborah Goodridge

Published by
Middleton Press
Easebourne Lane
Midhurst, West Sussex
GU29 9AZ
Tel: 01730 813169
Fax: 01730 812601

Printed & bound by Biddles Ltd,
Guildford and Kings Lynn

CONTENTS

ACKNOWLEDGEMENTS

We are grateful for the help received from many of the photographers mentioned in the caption credits. Sadly John Faulkner and Brian Moss, great authorities on the area, passed away during the preparation of this volume. We would like to express our gratitude for the assistance given by R.M.Casserley, D.Ewart, E.W.Fry, M.King, R.Kumar, N.Langridge, G.Lovell, D.Lovett, J.S.Petley, Mr D. & Dr S.Salter, Miss M.Wheeller and our ever helpful wives.

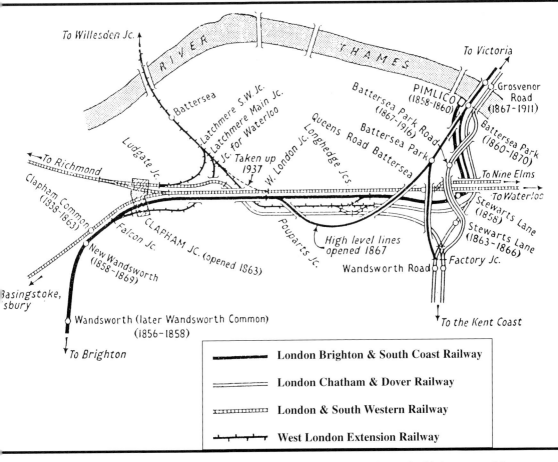

This map shows the original operating and/ or owning companies. The wider solid line was built by the West End of London & Crystal Palace Railway Company but always worked by the LBSCR. The WLER constructed the line from Kensington (now Olympia) but trains were run by different companies. It had joint ownership - London & North Western Railway (one third), Great Western Railway (one third), London & South Western Railway (one sixth) and London Brighton & South Coast Railway (one sixth). (Railway Magazine)

GEOGRAPHICAL SETTING

The station is situated at about 30ft above sea level on the eastern slope of the low clay hill which encompasses South London. This is penetrated by substantial cuttings west of the platforms; north thereof the tracks are on embankments and eastwards the lines are mostly on brick arches. Prior to urbanisation, the land had been largely devoted to market gardening, having earlier been marsh bordering the River Thames.

The station was built in the parish of Battersea which later became the Metropolitan Borough of Battersea. It seems that the name of Clapham, a village over one mile distant, was chosen owing to the larger number of "gentlemen" resident in that area.

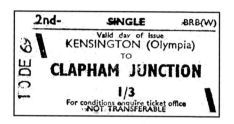

Diagram to illustrate the ownership of lines after the Grouping on 1st January 1923. (Railway Magazine)

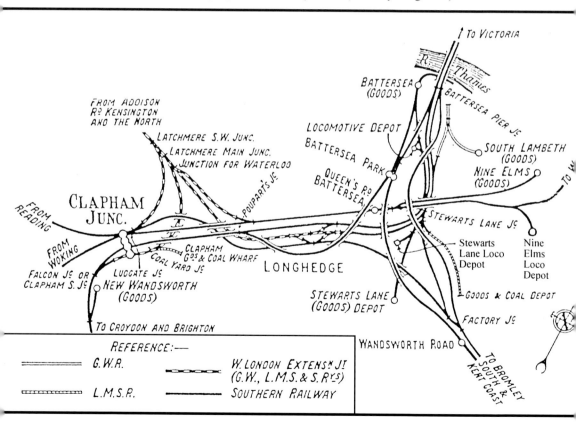

HISTORICAL BACKGROUND

The London & Southampton Railway opened between Woking (Common) and its London terminus at Nine Elms on 21st May 1838, a station called "Clapham Common" being provided west of the present platforms. The name was changed to the London & South Western Railway in 1839 and the line was extended to Waterloo (Bridge) in 1848, after which time Nine Elms became a goods depot. The LSWR line to Richmond opened in 1846.

It was to be over twenty years before another railway company appeared in the vicinity; this was the LBSCR which ran to Pimlico from 1858 to 1860 and to Victoria thereafter. LCDR services to Victoria also began in 1860.

The extension south of the West London Railway from Kensington on 2nd March 1863 coincided with the opening of Clapham Junction station and the four connecting lines shown on the map. The spur between Factory Junction and Longhedge Junction came into use on 1st July 1865 and the connection westwards to Ludgate Junction followed on 3rd August 1866. The LCDR High Level route to Victoria opened on 20th December of the same year. The WLR and the WLER combination became known as the West London Line.

The High Level route for LBSCR South London Line trains first saw traffic on 1st May 1867 and this was linked to Pouparts Junction on the 1st December following, completing the present main line between Clapham Junction and Victoria.

Alterations to the connections are detailed in the captions, as are recent changes to passenger services. The through routes became part of the Southern Railway in 1923 but the WLL remained in joint ownership. All the lines in the area became part of the Southern Region of British Railways upon Nationalisation in 1948, except the WLL which was allocated to the Western Region. It was transferred to the London Midland Region in 1970 and to the Southern Region in 1988.

Privatisation resulted in Railtrack being responsible for the station and other infrastructure. Trains from the station were operated thus - Victoria services by Connex South Central (from 26th May 1996), Waterloo services by South West Trains (from 4th February 1996) and the WLL by North London Railways (from 2nd March 1997). The dates given are those of the legal transfer although the names were in use prior to that.

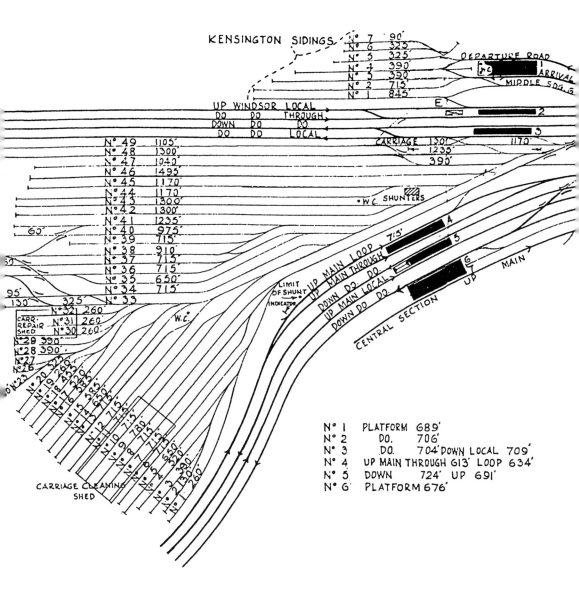

The control diagram for the South Western Section in 1948 shows the lengths of the sidings in feet, the platform numbers that were in use at that time and the locations of water columns (W.C.). The Central Section was simple in comparison and is revealed fully in the photographs.

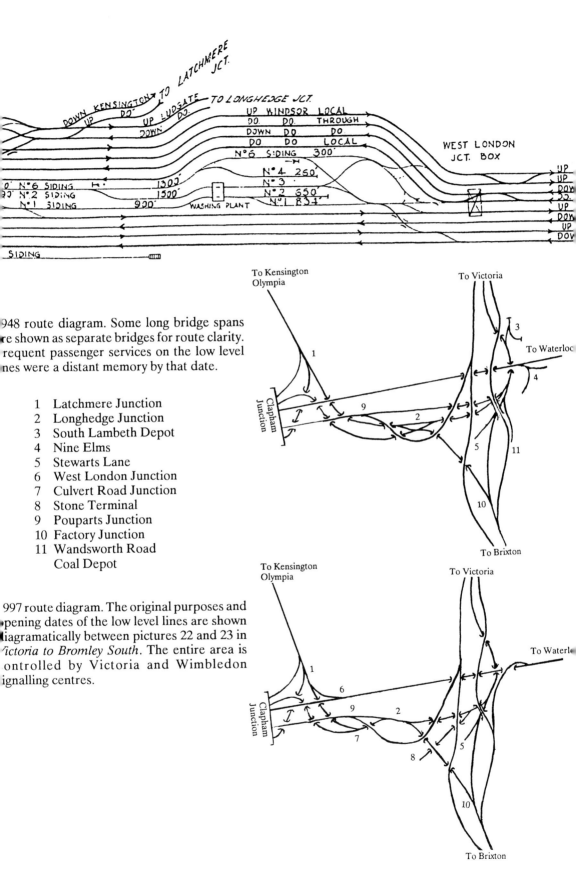

Top diagram labels:

TO LATCHMERE JCT.

DOWN KENSINGTON
UP DO.
UP LUDGATE DO.
TO LONGHEDGE JCT.
DOWN

UP WINDSOR LOCAL
DO. DO. THROUGH
DOWN DO DO.
DO DO LOCAL
Nº 6 SIDING 300'
Nº 4 250'
Nº 3
Nº 2 650'
Nº 1 834'

WEST LONDON
JCT. BOX

UP
UP
DOW
DO.
UP
DOWN
UP
DOW

DO' Nº 6 SIDING H·
DO' Nº 2 SIDING
Nº 1 SIDING
1300'
1500'
900'
WASHING PLANT

SIDING

---

948 route diagram. Some long bridge spans
re shown as separate bridges for route clarity.
requent passenger services on the low level
nes were a distant memory by that date.

1 Latchmere Junction
2 Longhedge Junction
3 South Lambeth Depot
4 Nine Elms
5 Stewarts Lane
6 West London Junction
7 Culvert Road Junction
8 Stone Terminal
9 Pouparts Junction
10 Factory Junction
11 Wandsworth Road
    Coal Depot

997 route diagram. The original purposes and
pening dates of the low level lines are shown
iagramatically between pictures 22 and 23 in
ictoria to Bromley South. The entire area is
ontrolled by Victoria and Wimbledon
ignalling centres.

To Kensington Olympia

To Victoria

To Waterloc

Clapham Junction

To Brixton

CLAPHAM JUNCTION 1948 to 1959

1. Class W 4-6-2T no. 1917 still carried the word SOUTHERN when photographed on 12th May 1949; change was slower in the days before stick-on vinyl lettering. It is working freight from the West London Line to Norwood Yard and is waiting for the signals to change. (J.H.Aston)

2. Pictured two months earlier on the same line, class H no. 31005 displays its new lettering, with the words well spaced. It had worked the last Saturday morning train from Kensington Olympia on 26th March and was about to back the coaches into Pig Hill sidings for the weekend. (J.H.Aston)

3. Inner suburban services were worked by first generation electric stock with wooden framed bodies well into the 1950s. Originally formed as 3-car units, they had a wider steel bodied coach added during the late 1940s. This such example is bound for Chessington South on 8th November 1949.(C.G.B.Herbert)

1950 PLATFORM RENUMBERING

South West Division		
New number		*Old number*
1	Kensington departures	1
2	Kensington arrivals	1
3	Up Windsor local	2
4	Up Windsor through	2
5	Down Windsor through	3
6	Down Windsor local	3
7	Up main loop	4
8	Up main through	4
9	Down main through	5
10	Up main local	5
11	Down main local	6

Central Division		
New number		*Old number*
12	Up through	7
13	Down through	8
14	Up local	9
15	Down local	10
16	Kensington departures	11
17	Kensington arrivals	12

4. The signalling at Nationalisation on the Brighton side was entirely mechanical, modernisation having been delayed by World War II. These are the up signals at the approach to the station. They vanished, along with the nearby "C" Box, on 12th October 1952. (N.L.Browne)

5. The service to Kensington Olympia had operated in peak hours only since 1941; this included Saturday midday in the era of the 5½ day working week. The trains were always noted for their unusual coaches - no.41291 is departing with an articulated set composed of two ex-SECR steam railcar saloons. (R.S.Carpenter coll.)

6. The Royal Train for Derby Day at Epsom Races in 1953 was hauled by "Schools" class no. 30915 *Brighton*, finished in lined black livery with white wheel rims. It made a change to see this class of locomotive and a female monarch here. The signal box on the right controlled the Brighton lines in the area and Falcon Junction from 1952 to 1980. (P.Hay)

7. There was almost constant activity in the carriage sidings between platforms 6 and 7 as every West of England, Bournemouth and Weymouth train returned here from Waterloo for servicing. Class E4 0-6-2T no. 32493 is coupled to a shunters truck formed from a former Beattie tender on a dull day in May 1954. Two or three Southampton boat trains were prepared each weekday. (D.Clayton)

8. The weather is bright as holidaymakers return from the South Coast to the Midlands behind no. 34047 *Callington* in the Summer of 1954. The short siding on the left was used by locomotives of West London Line trains terminating at platform 17. The water tank remained in place until 1972. (N.L.Browne)

9. Summer Saturdays in the 1950s brought the maximum number of inter-regional trains via the West London Line and a welcome change for loco spotters. Class N 2-6-0 no. 31812 has just avoided blowing off under the bridge while it waits to leave for Brighton from platform 17 on 30th July 1955. (E.Wilmshurst)

10. The everchanging scene at the east end of the station was enhanced by the varied make up of the milk trains. No. 35008 *Orient Line* is about to pass through platform 6 with the 3.45pm departure for the West of England via East Putney on 3rd August 1956. (D.Cullum)

11. Entering platform 3 on 6th February 1957 is one of the then new DEMUs for the Hastings line; it is running empty from Eastleigh to Ashford Works via East Putney. Known as Kensington Sidings, the lines on the right were mainly used for the sorting of milk trains. London destinations included Morden, Vauxhall, Kensington and Mottingham. The 1911 "E" Box became "C" on 8th February 1957. (N.W.Sprinks)

12. The panorama from the footbridge includes class M7 0-4-4T no. 30321. The Windsor lines are adjacent to the milk tankers on the right. One of the unremunerative shunting operations carried out each day was the reversal of the order of the nine portions of the "Atlantic Coast Express". (N.L.Browne)

13. One of the eyebrow-raising events of the 1950s was the transfer of some Pannier tanks from the Western Region in 1959. These were mainly used for empty carriage working to and from Waterloo. No. 4672 was recorded on one such duty on 14th October 1959, having just passed under the bridge carrying "A" Box. (J.Scrace)

Other changes in the 1950s

1951	Windsor/Weybridge trains began to call regularly.
1958	20 minute interval suburban services increased to 30.
	Epsom trains, began to call regularly.
	Horsham trains carried two extra coaches to the new Gatwick Airport.

14. An 18-coach special train from Oakley Junction to Lewes on 12th August 1960 required the services of no. 34086 *219 Squadron* and class U1 no. 31895. Several coaches would be beyond the other end of platform 3. (J.Scrace)

15. The point of divergence of the Central and South Western Divisions of the Southern Region was the location of this and the following photograph, taken on 7th June 1961. Class U1 no. 31900 is heading the 5.49pm Victoria to Oxted, while three 4COR units form the 5.50pm Waterloo to Portsmouth Harbour, first stop Guildford. (H.F.Wheeller)

16. The 6.0pm Waterloo to Exeter Central (first stop Basingstoke) accelerates away from the 40mph speed restriction through platform 9, as a train from the Sussex coast approaches platform 12. Trains climb at 1 in 338 towards Wimbledon. Very few passenger trains stopped at the "through" platforms (7-9) until the 1980s. (H.F.Wheeller)

17. Empty milk tanks arrive at platform 2 on a wet day in November 1962, probably from Mottingham in the south-east suburbs of London. Later, they would be propelled into Kensington sidings and form part of a train to the West of England. (E.Wilmshurst)

18. The RCTS/SLS Railtour on 2nd December 1962 was a farewell to the two remaining Beattie Well Tanks, both of which were subsequently preserved. They have just left platform 6 and are bound for Hampton Court - see picture 8 in our *Branch Lines around Effingham Junction*. Many local services had been worked by this class when new. (S.C.Nash)

19. The structure supporting "A" Box suffered corrosion failure on 10th May 1965, aggravated by the great weight of the superstructure and steel plates added during World War II to give some protection from bombs. We see temporary supports being erected the next day on the lines to platforms 1 and 2. For many months Kensington trains were diverted to use platforms 16 and 17. (J.Scrace)

20. Class 3 2-6-2T no. 82018 stands at platform 17 with the 5.8pm from Kensington Olympia on 28th June 1965. Severe corrosion of the bridge girder is evident, owing to lack of smoke deflectors. Parcels and passengers were segregated on the bridge and lifts were provided for the former. (J.Scrace)

21. Seen from platform 16 on 10th May 1966 is an afternoon train from Olympia, by that time the last local steam worked service in London. The class 4 2-6-4Ts were introduced in 1951 but were slow to be allocated to this area. The 1952 "B" Box is also evident, but the Falcon Lane LMR Goods Depot is obscured by the train. (H.C.Casserley)

22. The class 3s began to appear at Clapham Junction in 1963; no. 41319 is on the curve from Latchmere Junction and approaches platform 2 on 6th July 1967, four days before the end of steam. Note the GWR-style distant signal, a legacy from the past joint ownership of the WLER. (R.E.Ruffell)

23. Plenty of advisers look on as a parcels van is rerailed at the London end of platform 3 on 26th September 1967. Such activity made a change for the numerous railway observers who frequented this end of the station, although they were fewer with the end of steam traction. (R.E.Ruffell)

24. Corridor coaches crammed every crevice on 30th April 1969. In the left background is the carriage repair shed into which sidings 30 to 32 were extended. In the right distance, alongside siding 49, is the Signal & Telegraph Training School. The frequency of boat trains diminished in the 1960s, as most intercontinental passengers took to the air. (R.E.Ruffell)

Other changes in the 1960s

1963	Pullman cars withdrawn from boat trains
1964	Long distance milk traffic moved to the Western Region
1967	Twelve carriage sidings electrified
1968	Kingston Roundabout services curtailed to Kingston via Richmond
	Platforms 16 and 17 electrified
	Falcon Lane Goods Depot closed
1969	Transfer siding between Central and South Western Divisions taken out of use.

CLAPHAM JUNCTION - 1970s

25. "Western" class diesel no. 1025 stands under the repaired bridge at platform 17 on 9th May 1970 with freight from Severn Tunnel Junction bound for Norwood. The conductor rails allowed the platforms to be used for terminating trains in the event of the closure of Victoria. (R.E.Ruffell)

26. An eastward panorama on 28th April 1976 features two trains composed of steel bodied 4SUBS which monopolised local services on the Central and South Western Divisions for about forty years. Note that "A" Box had lost its steel plate roof but retained its wartime framing. The black arch in the distance is the pre-war carriage washing machine. (R.E.Ruffell)

27. No. 45110 was recorded on 8th June 1976 working a train from the Kent coalfield at Shepherdswell to Brent. It has been taken off the passenger lines into siding 49 from which branched sidings 50 to 52, close to Wandsworth Town station. The change in freight workings has always been worthy of study at this location. (R.E.Ruffell)

28. A May 1977 panorama from the footbridge includes some of the electrified sidings, the distinctive white markers on the repair shed doors and a Windsor line train in the right background. Seven trains for newspapers and/or mails left the yard each evening, one including a TPO for Weymouth. The yard also sorted a large number of parcels vans. (R.E.Ruffell)

30. No. 74001 arrives in the yard with empty boat train stock on 17th May 1977. The cleaners had a great variety of carriages to deal with. The locomotive was one of a small batch built for the Kent Coast electrification as class 71 and later converted to electro-diesel as class 74. (R.E.Ruffell)

29. A change from routine occurred on 29th May 1977 when one of the Waterloo & City line coaches came to the surface. They were taken to Eastleigh Works for periodic overhaul, sandwiched between special adaptor wagons. (R.E.Ruffell)

31. A notably short train appeared that day. It was being used for guard training. No. 33102 is providing the power; it could be driven from the end of the coach. The Bournemouth-Weymouth service was operating similarly, but with four coaches, from 1967. (R.E.Ruffell)

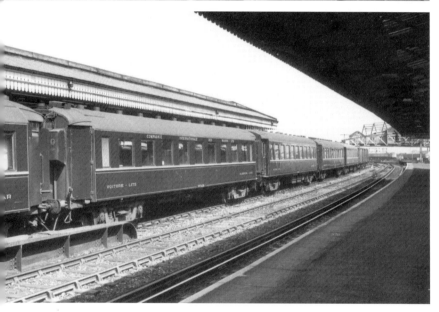

32. The "Night Ferry" coaches ran betwen Paris and Victoria, where they were normally serviced during the day. Each berth was supplied with lifebelts and each coach had its own coal-fired central heating system, which continued to burn when in the hold of the ship. Foreign mail vans are at the rear. The photo was taken in May 1979 and the service ceased on 31st October 1980. (R.E.Ruffell)

Other changes in the 1970s

1970	Falcon Lane sidings lifted
1970-73	Connections between Waterloo and Victoria lines in place but little used
1978	Mid-Sussex trains began to call regularly
1979	Reading trains began to call regularly
	Twice daily Manchester-Brighton starts

CLAPHAM JUNCTION - 1980s

33. A May 1980 photograph shows platform 17 to be roofless and devoid of name boards, despite the fact that trains from Manchester had been calling there for 12 months. The 1968 conductor rails show no signs of use; they extended to the signal box, the one on the left going a little further to enable trains to use the crossover there when necessary - see picture 42. (D.Clayton)

34. The Royal Train stands empty behind no. 33042 on 17th March 1981 as it waits to return to its base at Wolverton. Waiting at platform 4 on its way from Kingston to Waterloo is no. 508029. The class 508 stock had been introduced in 1979, replacing the 4PEP units which had appeared in the mid-1970s. (J.Scrace)

35. The 06.40 from Salisbury passes through platform 8 on 9th August 1982, hauled by no. 50021. Much of the fleet of these Mk.II coaches was based in the adjacent yard. There had been a covered passage from the footbridge to St. Johns Hill until truncated by bombing in the early 1940s. The remnant was used as a classroom until severely damaged by fire on 9th July 1981 and subsequently demolished. (J.Scrace)

36. No. 73114 had been set aside in the yard with its cement train on 15th March 1983. The supplementary diesel engine on these electric locomotives was useful on such occasions. No. 33101 is probably arriving with empty stock. Much of that on view is of the Mk I variety. Mail and newspaper trains ceased in 1988. (R.E.Ruffell)

←——————

37. Restored to its original livery (apart from the yellow end), 4SUB no. 4732 was working the 12.43 Victoria to Beckenham Junction when recorded on 15th April 1983. It is passing "B" Box which had been taken out of use on 16th November 1980 but still retained its name. (J.Scrace)

←——————

38. A telescopic view on 22nd September 1983 features no. 33103 with the 16.49 from Kensington Olympia with a 4TC set. These unmotored sets had a driving compartment at each end so the locomotive could propel the train back unmanned. The space on the left had carried the line to platform 1 but this had been taken out of use on 13th April 1980. (C.Wilson)

39. The 12.55 Waterloo to Portsmouth Harbour was formed of one of the class 412 units on 10th June 1986. Built as class 410 in 1957-59 for use in Kent, some of the units were refurbished in 1982. Their harsh suspension and thin cushions left a lot to be desired. "A" Box was struck by fire on 15th June 1986, resulting in severe delays and cancellations. (C.Wilson)

40. A rare interlude in the clatter of passing trains was recorded in December 1986. The picture reveals the limited clearance at the foot of the ramp and that a barrier had been erected between the running line and the sidings. Most of the subway was then closed for renovation and work had started on a new entrance at its south end. (A.C.Mott)

42. In ScotRail livery, no. 47469 *Glasgow Chamber of Commerce* climbs up the gradient to plaform 17 with the 11.55 from Manchester on 18th June 1987. It became increasingly difficult to find reliable locomotives to work this twice daily service. This one is obscuring our view of the 1980 Victoria Signalling Centre. The van in Pig Hill sidings is probably a cripple. (J.Scrace)

41. A further change in rolling stock for the popularly known "Kenny Belle" was pictured on 13th May 1987 as a DMU rounds the curve to platform 2. It was this little used line that later received attention from Irish terrorists who presumably thought that their explosive device would paralyse Clapham Junction. (J.Scrace)

43. The aftermath of the so-called "Clapham Disaster" was photographed the day after the collision as no. 73129 removed the rear coach of the class 423 on 13th December 1988. There were 35 deaths and a large number of injuries when a rear-end impact was followed by a passing train hitting the wreckage. A wiring error in the signalling was the primary cause. (F.Hornby)

CLAPHAM JUNCTION to 1997

44. No. 73130 is at the front of the 09.02 to Olympia on 11th July 1990 and no. 73136 is at the rear, probably due to the available driver not being qualified for push-pull working. The curve to Latchmere Junction had been singled on 25th May 1990. The overgrown Kensington sidings are in the distance; they had been retained for the engineers. (J.Scrace)

Other changes in the 1980s

The following services began to call -

1984	**Littlehampton and Hastings**
1985	**Basingstoke/Alton**
1985	**Guildford via Cobham**
1986	**Bournemouth semi-fast**
1987	**East Grinstead (electric thereon)**
1988	**Salisbury semi-fast**
1989	**Portsmouth semi-fast**

45. An up train from Portsmouth departs from platform 7 while a down service enters no. 9 on 2nd November 1991. Up non-stop trains passed through no. 8 these included Portsmouth fasts and trains from Weymouth and west of Salisbury. The other regular non-stop services passed through South Central platforms and were the expresses to Brighton and to Gatwick Airport. (V.Mitchell)

46. No. 59003 *Yeoman Highlander* is entering platform 16 on 9th March 1992 in order to reach the West London Line with its train of empty stone wagons en route from Crawley to Merehead Quarry in Somerset. This class of locomotive made a change here, being privately owned and American built. (J.Scrace)

47. Three trains accelerate from their stops at the station on 23rd April 1992. Nearest is the 16.45 Waterloo to Poole (semi-fast Bournemouth trains having been extended there since 1988); in the background is the 16.51 Victoria to Hastings (front eight coaches to Eastbourne only), while a class 455 is in the middle, destined for the suburbs. (C.Wilson)

48. Making a change to the scene on 24th April 1993 are class 465 "Networker" units, awaiting delivery to Kent. Alongside is no. 60016 and near that is no. 56001. In the background is no. 33030 working a railtour called "The Scratcher". The carriage repair shed had been demolished in July 1992. (P.G.Barnes)

49. Attached to the "Queen of Scots" and other privately owned coaches on 1st October 1994 is no. 73107 *Redhill 1844-1994*. The siding numbers are shown on the footbridge; electrified at that time were nos 9-13, 40 and 44-49. (P.G.Barnes)

50. The 07.45 from Poole creeps into platform 7 on 1st January 1994 owing to the severe curvature. The use of this platform instead of no. 8 (left) is due to the better sighting for guard and platform staff prior to departure. The former milk docks are right of centre. Two of these five-car class 442 "Wessex" units are slightly too long for platform 7, so the doors of the rear set have to remain locked! (V.Mitchell)

51. A major change took place on 31st May 1994 with the reintroduction of a Clapham Junction-Willesden Junction service after an inexcusable interval of 54 years. Elderly DMUs had to be used owing to the incomplete electrification of the route. Seen on the first day, no. L721 had to use platform 17 owing to a points failure on the route to its allocated platform, no. 2. (M.Turvey)

52. Owing to staff shortages and ageing stock, the service was unreliable. Only a single car could be found on 12th July 1995 to work one of the two trains needed to provide the 30-minute interval service. The nearby conductor rail was provided in 1993 and used from July of that year until May 1994. Permanent electric services commenced on 1st October 1996. (M.Turvey)

53. Steam made a rare appearance on Sunday 11th February 1996, when class S15 no. 828 ran from Portsmouth Harbour to platform 6, via Herne Hill. It is seen entering siding 49 after reversal; later it departed from platform 9 and returned via Cobham. (V.Mitchell)

54. Our DMU has just left platform 2 on 3rd August 1996 and is about to turn left at Ludgate Junction. This unexpected name dates from 1866, when the LSWR commenced a service from Hounslow to Ludgate Hill via Loughborough Junction for workers in the City. The crossovers are mainly used by freight trains. (V.Mitchell)

55. Eurostar services to Paris and Brussels from Waterloo commenced on 14th November 1994 but Clapham Yard was not long enough to be used for servicing the 18-vehicle trains. However, one of the shorter North of London Eurostars was recorded at rest between test runs on 2nd October 1996. Each end three bogies are motored; the others are articulated - two coaches on each one. (P.G.Barnes)

56. Most of the wooden platform buildings from the alterations of 1907-08 were still in place when photo nos. 56 to 59 were taken on 23rd September 1997. Dual voltage no. 313007 is about to leave platform 2 for Willesden Junction at 12.27. (V.Mitchell)

57. Three-car class 159 DMUs were introduced on Waterloo-Exeter services in May 1993, each vehicle being powered unlike earlier 3-car diesel units. The entire fleet was based at a new depot at Salisbury; thus Clapham Junction no longer serviced long distance trains. This is the 12.41 departure. The bridge panels devoid of rivets indicate the site of the former footway to St. Johns Hill. (V.Mitchell)

58. The Victoria Area Signalling Centre was opened on 17th May 1980 and has been gradually expanded so that by 1997 its control extended northwards to North Pole Depot and fringed with the Waterloo Area Signalling Centre, which had taken over the Nine Elms-Clapham Junction section on 27th May 1990. Southwards the panels controlled South Central lines to fringe with Three Bridges and eastwards to London Bridge panels. The Centre also controls south-east routes from

Victoria. This montage of views commences with a look westwards from the Centre, with the former "B" Box in the join of the pages. Graffiti is prolific in the area, despite the presence of full time platform staff and train drivers having radios. The evidence has been removed from these photographs in order not to perpetrate this evil practice. They were taken on 23rd September 1997. (V.Mitchell)

◄——————— The LBSCR entrance was in St. Johns Hill and had been recently restored, although no longer used as such. The rear of the building is seen in pictures 1, 20 and 59. The platform signs proclaimed *CLAPHAM JUNCTION. BRITAIN'S BUSIEST RAILWAY STATION.* (V.Mitchell)

The 13.35 Waterloo to Gillingham (Dorset) creeps away from platform 9, the leading DMU being no. 159019. The rear part would be detached at Salisbury. The waste land between the pages was the site of a sub-station containing rotary convertors. Electricity at 11kV AC was generated at the former LSWR power station at

———————➤ The bomb damage inflicted during World War II had still not been repaired and passengers on the busy platforms 9 and 10 had limited weather protection. There was a similar canopy deficiency on platforms 7 and 8. (V.Mitchell)

Durnsford Road, Wimbledon, until 1958. It was reduced to 660 volts DC locally. Leaving platform 15 is a local train for South London, with a two-car class 456 leading. The stone pillar on the right marks the position of the LSWR entrance, the passage from which passed over the sub-station. (V.Mitchell)

59. Connex South Central began a weekday Gatwick Airport-Rugby service on 1st June 1997, using class 319 dual-voltage units. This gave three trains per hour to Olympia. On Sundays, an hourly Clapham Junction-Watford Junction service was provided. (V.Mitchell)

Other changes in the 1990s

1990	Booking office refurbished on north side
	Mid-Sussex trains carried a Southampton portion which ran via Hove from 1991 and was extended to Bournemouth in 1994
1991	Kingston Roundabout service restored
	Portsmouth via Fareham trains (introduced 1990) began to call
1993	Paignton became a new destination and Exeter trains began to call regularly
1997	Brighton-Manchester trains ceased to call
	3-portion trains began (Bournemouth, Littlehampton and Eastbourne

STEWARTS LANE

60. The site was heavily bombed during World War II and relics of the SR were still to be seen in 1949. Set aside at that time was this unusual civil engineers inspection car.
(Wessex coll.)

61. Smoke, coal dust and ash always filled the air at this location near the arches carrying South London Line trains, which was recorded in August 1950. Ten-ton coal wagons were hoisted to the top of the coaling plant and tipped into its hopper.
(Wessex coll.)

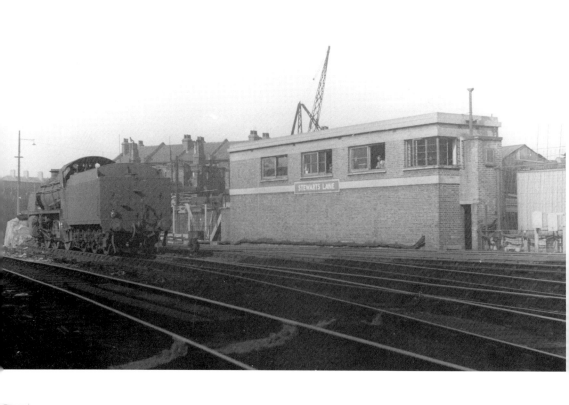

62. Another photograph from the same period shows the box that controlled access to the depot and the junction on the former LCDR Low Level lines. The bridge carrying the Waterloo lines is on the left; the locomotive is on the headshunt between the coaling plant and the engine shed. The signal box was in use until 17th May 1980. (Wessex coll.)

64. Pictured on 29th September 1951 is "Britannia" class no. 70014 *Iron Duke* ready for one of the depot's prestigious services. It was the London depot for all the Kent Coast services until they began to be electrified in 1959. (R.S.Carpenter)

63. From the same era is a photograph of class H no.1263 alongside the carriage washing plant. This northward view includes the ex-LCDR High Level lines to Victoria, a footbridge passing under them and the ex-LSWR main line bridge in the background. (Wessex coll.)

65. The view from a South London train on 23rd May 1953 included two Eastern Region class B1 4-6-0s deputising for SR Pacifics withdrawn following a crank axle failure at Crewkerne. The fan of sixteen shed roads is in the haze on the right. (N.W.Sprinks)

66. Pullman cars for the Kent Coast services, including the "Golden Arrow" were kept in the grimy environs of "The Lane". Shunting on 15th September 1957 was P class no. 31558, which was withdrawn in 1960 and broken up. Parts of the former LCDR Longhedge Locomotive Works remained standing. (R.C.Riley)

67. The footbridge seen in picture 63 was the viewpoint for this picture of two locomotives selected to become part of the National Collection and now in the custody of the National Railway Museum. They are class T3 4-4-0 no. 593 and ex-LBSCR "Terrier" class no. 82 *Boxhill*. The date is 27th April 1958. (S.C.Nash)

68. Photographed a few minutes later from behind *Boxhill* was class 20 no. D8817 with a van train. Rationalisation eventually reduced the four tracks to one. Diesel and electric locomotives infiltrated the depot from 1959 and steam vanished during 1963. (S.C.Nash)

69. Part of the Stewarts Lane complex was adapted for use by the new fleets of electric locomotives. Seen on 16th July 1967 are two class 73 electro-diesels and one of the small batch of electric locomotives built for use in Kent. They were employed on the "Golden Arrow" in its final years and on goods trains; a pantograph was provided for use in a limited number of sidings fitted with overhead wires. (R.S.Carpenter)

70. The electric maintenance shed housed class 73s on 4th January 1968. Some were built with straight sides for use on the restricted clearances of the Hastings main line, while others were of normal profile. Two such (nos. E6103 and E6102) are in the background being prepared for trial running. (R.E.Ruffell)

71. A general view across the site of the steam running shed in 1994 includes two rows of class 33 diesels set aside for repair or scrapping and a line of class 73 electro-diesels. All but five members of this class were based at this depot at this time. (F.Hornby)

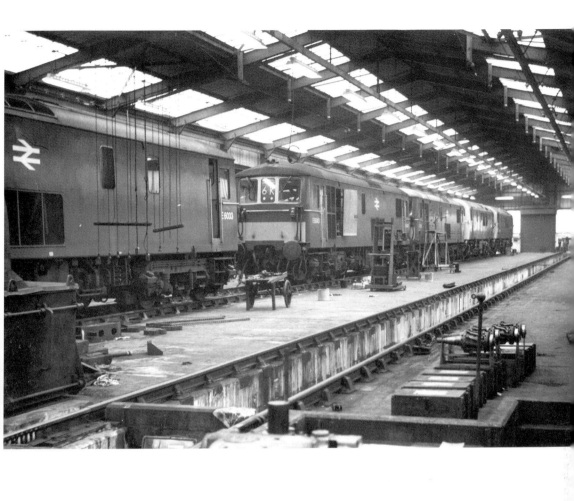

72. The fuel tanks were placed near the site of the old coaling plant, in the shadow of the Atlantic Line viaduct which mainly carried South London Line trains. Two class 47s throb as a class 33 stands under an arch on 10th April 1994. Railway accountants were soon to prove that it was cheaper

to convey diesel oil to depots by road. Freight has to be put on our highways before grants can be made to remove it. (M.J.Stretton)

73. The caption number reflects the class of no. 73208 *Croydon 1883-1983* which is in Gatwick Express livery and stands on the line to that organisation's carriage sheds on a dull day in February 1996. The offices and wall on the left were once part of the steam running shed. From 1991, the official name was "Battersea Stewarts Lane". (M.Turvey)

4. The fleet of air-conditioned Mk. II Gatwick Express coaches were allocated an exclusive maintenance shed when the non-stop 24-hour service was introduced in 1984. No. 73003 is coupled to a spare set. All trains have a class 489 GLV at the oppposite end to the locomotive to provide extra power, generous luggage space and a return driving position. The Stewarts Lane goods depot had occupied part of this site until it closed on 22nd November 1970. (M.J.Stretton)

75. The maintenance shed was kept to almost clinical standards and massive exhaust extractors were provided. Waiting attention on 4th June 1996 was no. 60001 *Steadfast* and no. 73101 *The Royal Alex* in smart Pullman livery. Due for examination on the left is no. 73138. (M.J.Stretton)

NINE ELMS

76. The locomotive depot was the largest on the LSWR and was subject to steady decline in the SR and BR eras. A westward view through smoke haze in September 1960 shows all of the 15-road 1889 shed and part of the 11-road 1910 structure. All the roads converged on a 65ft turntable left of the camera. (R.S.Carpenter)

77. A close up on 7th October 1965 reveals the difference in roof styles of the two sheds. The row of rivetted columns indicates the original extent of the Old Shed. No. 35022 *Holland-America Line* is clear but the other locomotives are shrouded in the resident pollutants. (T.Heavyside)

78. No. 34087, devoid of its *145 Squadron* nameplates, is about to climb up the curve to the main lines which pass under Loco Junction signal box, visible in the background. The points on the right served the south part of Nine Elms goods depot, which closed on 29th July 1968. (T.Heavyside)

79. The coaling plant hopper had chutes over two roads and was in use from 1923 to 1967. Class 5 4-6-0 no. 73065 was one of a number of BR Standard locomotives allocated here to work with a small group of ex-SR machines to the end of steam. (T.Heavyside)

81. Colour light signals stand out in the dusk as participants on a 4EPB railtour travelled over the new Lindford Street curve, a route normally restricted to Eurostar trains. On the right is the site of Nine Elms steam sheds, redeveloped as the New Covent Garden fruit and vegetable market, but shamefully devoid of railway sidings. (V.Mitchell)

80. Brookland Road had the gates to paradise in the eyes of many young engine admirers. Sadly the gates were to shut permanently in July 1967 when steam traction ceased in London. The photograph was taken on 13th May of that year, as were the previous two. (T.Heavyside)

LOW LEVEL LINES

82. Class H2 no. 32426 was moving empty coaches from Polegate to Halwill on 27th July 1954 and has just passed under the former LBSCR High Level route to Victoria to reach the railwaymen's allotments at Longhedge Junction. (S.C.Nash)

83. Looking in the same direction but from the other side of the quadruple track, we witness the passing of H class no. 31005 with empty milk tanks from Stewarts Lane to Kensington on the same day. This train was often worked by one of the small P class 0-6-0s. (S.C.Nash)

84. This and the next view of Longhedge Junction are in the opposite direction and were taken in August 1956. Class U1 no. 31904 is standing with a Luton to Brighton excursion while ex-LMS class 5 no. 44863 is passing with day trippers from Rugby to Margate. The bridge also carries the Victoria line over the tracks - see map II. (S.C.Nash)

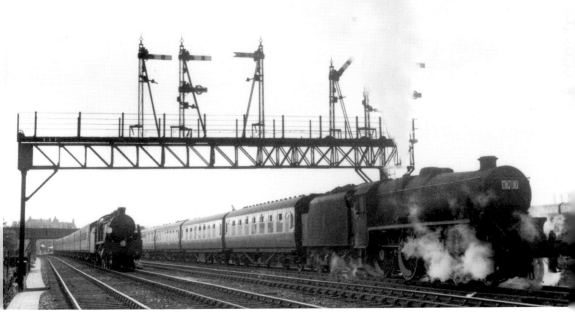

85. The pair of lines on the left pass under all the main lines to reach the northern (Windsor) platforms at Clapham Junction. The adjacent pair also run under the main lines but continue to Latchmere

Junction and the West London Line. Behind the signal box are the lines to Pouparts Junction. The box at the latter closed on 27th October 1952 and that at the former on 23rd July 1978. (A.E. Bennett)

86. Passing behind Longhedge Junction box and rising to Pouparts Junction on 11th August 1956 is class K no. 32339 with the 5.10pm from Battersea Yard to Norwood Junction. The signal gantry on the right also appears in the previous three pictures. (J.J.Smith)

87. A southward view on 9th July 1966 features the Low Level lines at Battersea and the bridge carrying the main lines to Waterloo. The left pair of electrified tracks are Eastern Division and the right pair are Central Division. The other lines were for freight to and from Battersea Yard. The LT stock was for use on the Isle of Wight and is seen having just reversed on its journey from Wimbledon to Stewarts Lane. (J.J.Smith)

88. Looking west from the South London Line in the winter of 1968-69 we see a breakdown crane in action on the Victoria High Level route and new ballast under the bullhead rails of the Eastern division tracks. The curved lines on the left are from Factory Junction to Longhedge Junction. The sidings below them were once part of Longhedge Works and by the 1980s, one was in use as a stone terminal. Tarmac usually received one train per week in 1997. (J.J.Smith)

89. The second map indicates the boundary points of line ownership and gives details of the joint ownership of the WLER. The post was still to be seen in 1974. Changes on 4th May 1969 meant the newly ballasted lines were merged east of Longhedge Junction and other alterations made west thereof. (J.Scrace)

90. This location is north of that seen in picture 87. The four Low Level running lines are on the left and are starting their stiff climb to Grosvenor Bridge. In the foreground is part of Battersea Yard which ceased to receive goods traffic on 4th May 1970. On the Eastern Division High Level line on 25th March 1981 is an up boat train with an MLV (Motor Luggage Van) leading. Battersea Yard box had closed on 24th July 1966; access to the yard was controlled from Stewarts Lane box. (F.Hornby)

The Southern Electric Group ran the "End of an Era Railtour" on 15th April 1995 with 4EPBs nos 5001 and 5176, to mark the demise of the class 415 slam-door stock. These units, along with the closely related 4SUBs, had served the area well for almost 50 years. The itinerary shows the mileage, platform numbers and times. The train used the Low Level lines more than once and gave a rare opportunity to record the scene from an open window.

London Bridge to Charing Cross "End of an Era" Railtour

Miles	Location	Time
.00	LONDON BGE Dep	09.00
	Borough Mkt Jn	09/01
0.57	Cannon St (7) Arr	09.03
	Dep	09.10
1.19	Metropolitan Jn	09/12
	Blackfriars Carr Road	09/14
2.03	BLACKFRIARS (1)	09.16
	Dep	09.22
5.10	Loughborough Jn	09/27
5.52	Canterbury Rd Jn	09/28
5.68	Brixton	09/30
	Shepherds Lane Jn	09/31
7.07	Voltaire Road Jn	09/32
7.54	Stewarts Lane Jn	09/34
8.19	Battersea Pier Jn	09/36
9.10	VICTORIA (5) Arr	09.40
	Dep	09.50
10.09	Battersea Pier Jn	09/52
10.46	Stewarts Lane Jn	09/54
10.76	Longhedge Jn	09/57
12.04	CLAPHAM JN Arr	10.00
	Dep	10.10
13.12	Longhedge Jn	10/13
13.51	Factory Jn	10/14
13.75	Voltaire Road Jn	10/15 AL
14.78	Crofton Road Jn	10/18
18.67	Nunhead	10/21
20.27	Lewisham	10/26
	Catford Bridge	10/29
23.67	New Beckenham	10/31
25.30	Elmers End	10/35
27.20	ADDISCOMBE (2) Arr	10.40
	Dep	10.55
	WOODSIDE Arr	10.57
	Dep	11.07
29.10	Elmers End	11/10
30.53	NEW BECKENHAM	11.13
	Dep	11.21
31.35	Beckenham Jn	11/24
32.39	Shortlands Jn	11/26
34.74	Bickley Jn	11/31
35.67	Petts Wood Jn	11/33
37.24	ORPINGTON (5) Arr	11.35
	Dep	11.49
45.48	Sevenoaks	11/59
53.01	TONBRIDGE (2) Arr	12.09
	Dep	12.17
	Godstone	12/34
72.57	REDHILL (2) Arr	12.49
	Dep	12.54
	Godstone	13/00
92.33	Tonbridge	13/17
97.56	PADDOCK WOOD	13.30
	Dep	13.48
107.26	Maidstone West	14/03
	AYLESFORD Arr	14.08
	Dep	14.24
118.51	STROOD Arr	14.35
	Dep	14.45
118.74	Rochester Bge Jn	14/47
	No 1 Down Sdg	14/48
121.08	GILLINGHAM Arr	14.54/15.02
129.72	SITTINGBOURNE	15.10
	(Plat 3) Dep	15.18
131.63	Kemsley	15/21
135.65	Queenborough Arr	15.28
	Dep	15.31
137.63	SHEERNESS Arr	15.35
	Dep	16.00
139.59	Queenborough	16/04
	Kemsley	16/12
145.35	Western Jn	16/14
	NEWINGTON Arr	16.17
	Dep	16.26
153.31	GILLINGHAM Dep	16.36
155.44	Rochester Bdge Jn	16/38
155.67	Strood	16/40
161.66	Gravesend	16/50
169.49	Dartford	17/03
169.76	Dartford Jn	17/04
174.68	Sidcup	17/12
178.68	Lee	17/17
	Lee Spur Jn	17/19
181.01	Grove Park	17/28
182.50	BROMLEY NORTH	17.33
	Plat 2	17.45
184.19	Grove Park	17/51
186.01	Hither Green	17/54
186.48	Parks Bridge Jn	17/56
187.07	Lewisham	17/58
188.73	Nunhead	18/05
191.00	Cambria Jn	18/09
191.56	Brixton Jn	18/12
192.29	Linford St	18/15
192.69	Nine Elms Jn	18/17
194.69	WATERLOO (19)	18.22
	Dep	18.37
196.69	Nine Elms Jn	18/42
198.05	West London Jn	18/44
198.45	Latchmere Jn	18/46
201.28	KENSINGTON O	18.58
	Dep	19.06
204.11	Latchmere Jn	19/09
204.75	Longhedge Jn	19/12
205.35	Factory Jn	19/14
205.50	Voltaire Rd Jn	19/15
208.16	Crofton Road Jn	19/18
209.26	Nunhead	19/21
211.12	Lewisham	19/26
211.51	Parks Bridge Jn	19/28
212.31	Hither Green	19/30
213.01	Lee	19/31
217.08	Sidcup	19/38
227.36	Crayford Spur B	19/42
228.06	Crayford Creek Jn	19/44
234.47	Plumstead	19/51
237.04	Charlton	19/57
240.23	North Kent E Jn	20/07
241.57	Spa Road	20/09
242.58	LONDON BDGE	20.13
	DEP	20.14
243.17	Metropolitan Jn	20/15
243.67	WATERLOO E	20.17
	Dep	20.18
244.48	CHARING X	20.20

91. Having descended from Factory Junction (named after the LCDR's locomotive works), the train is about to pass under the main line from Kent to Victoria. The location is in the left background of picture 65. On the right are berthing sidings. Beyond the arches, Wandsworth Road London Midland Region goods depot had been in use until 30th April 1973. It had been opened by the Midland Railway in 1874. (V.Mitchell)

92. Crossing to the other side of the train quickly, we have the opportunity to look back at part of the diesel depot and at the washing machine. The locomotive on the left is on the line to the area used for the Gatwick Expresses and seen in picture 74. (V.Mitchell)

93. Seconds later we glimpse the remainder of the diesel depot through the adjacent span. The arches carrying the South London Line trains are in the background. The prestigious Venice Simplon Orient Express coaches were based at Stewarts Lane. (V.Mitchell)

94. A few more seconds elapse and the Battersea Reversible Line comes into view. This replaced the four tracks (seen in pictures 65, 67 and 68) in 1978. The alterations meant that trains could run direct between Pouparts Junction and Factory Junction for the first time. Some Victoria-Tunbridge Wells trains used this route to reduce congestion on the main line; they ran non-stop through Clapham Junction but were discontinued in September 1997. (V.Mitchell)

95. Turning quickly to look forwards we see the convergance of the Battersea Reversible and on the left is the original route which led to the short lived Pimlico terminus. The hollow shell of Battersea Power Station still awaited a use that might benefit the railways. (V.Mitchell)

96. A short distance further north, the Low Level route passes under Battersea Park Road before starting its steep climb to cross the River Thames. The non-electrified lines were little used and once led to the wharf, goods yard and LBSCR engine sheds. On the other side had been the Western Region South Lambeth goods depot. Opened by the GWR as a milk

depot in 1910, it accepted goods from 1911. It was transferred to the Southern Region and renamed "Nine Elms" in 1968 and was used for signal rewiring trains in the early 1980s, having been closed to general traffic on 1st November 1980. (V.Mitchell)

97. At the same location, but looking south on the return journey from Victoria, we have a glimpse of the lofty Nine Elms flyover, opened in 1994 to enable Eurostar trains to run between the former LCDR and LSWR routes. (V.Mitchell)

LATCHMERE JUNCTION

98. Latchmere Junction box was situated by Main Junction. Having run through platform 16 and passed under the main lines, Q class no. 33017 is proceeding with the 12.40pm Brighton to Birmingham train on 31st July 1954. The locomotive would be replaced with a more suitable one at Kensington Olympia. (J.J.Smith)

99. The rear coach of this troop train is on South Western Junction, a reference to the railway company to which the curve was first connected. The train was running from Harwich (Parkestone Quay) to Aldershot on 5th August 1956. The Eastern Region coaches were hauled on the final part of their journey by class U no. 31624. (J.J.Smith)

100. Looking towards Kensington in 1956, we see Main Junction by the box and South West Junction in the background. Note the relative levels of the two diverging routes. The box closed on 24th April 1983 after which time the junctions were simply numbered 1 and 2 in the order of viewing. (A.E.Bennett)

101. The houses of Latchmere Road are in the background as class M7 no. 30319 passes Latchmere Junction starting signal on the curve to platform 17 on 12th June 1959. The train is the 5.6pm from Olympia and it includes four former SECR 100-seat coaches. (J.J.Smith)

102. The connection between the West London and Waterloo lines, lifted in 1936, was reinstated on 15th November 1992. It was for use by empty Eurostar trains between Waterloo and their North Pole Depot and for their connecting services. No. 3206 is running over the new Latchmere no. 3 junction on 13th July 1995. From east to west, the junctions are thus illogically numbered 3, 1, 2. (F.Hornby)

103. Known as Sheepcote Curve, the new connection is seen from a train on the up main line to Waterloo in January 1997. The routes join at West London Junction; the curve and the lines to Mitre Bridge Junction, beyond North Pole Depot, are signalled for reversible running. Waterloo International was officially opened on 17th May 1993 but not brought into use until 14th November 1994, owing to delays with the Channel Tunnel. (V.Mitchell)

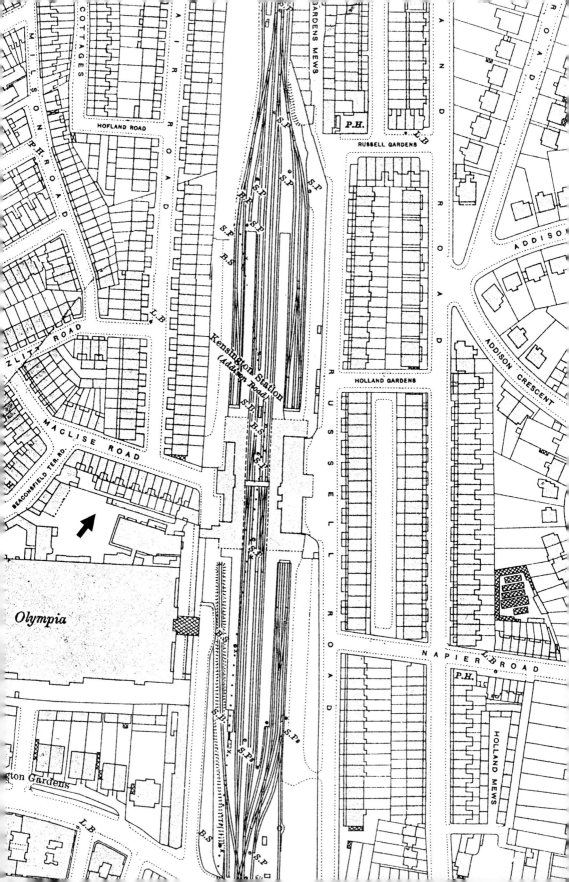

KENSINGTON OLYMPIA

The 1916 Ordnance Survey at 25ins to 1 mile is included as the track layout changed little until the 1980s. North, Middle and South signal boxes are marked (S.B.), as are the extensive buildings and canopies which were severely damaged during World War II. For most of the era of this book, the only local BR service was to Clapham Junction and so it is appropriate to include the station herein. Regular passenger trains to Clapham Junction had been withdrawn on 21st October 1940 due to the effects of bombing and to the need to give priority to wartime traffic. However, two peak hour journeys were retained, unadvertised, primarily for use by staff at the Post Office Savings Bank. The public was also carried but the trains did not appear in the timetables until 5th May 1969, apart from the period 18th June 1951 to 11th June 1956. As traffic was increasing, four return trips on Monday to Friday mornings and evenings were introduced on 16th May 1983. From 14th May 1990, the number was increased to seven at each end of the working day, this including the two Manchester-Brighton services. A half-hourly all day service between Clapham Junction and Willesden Junction was provided on Mondays to Fridays from 31st May 1994. It was extended to Saturdays in May 1995. The frequency between Kensington Olympia and Clapham Junction was further enhanced when an hourly Gatwick Airport-Rugby service was introduced on 2nd June 1997, weekdays only. On Sundays there were hourly trains between Watford Junction and Clapham Junction but the InterCity trains no longer called at Clapham Junction.

104. The station had been named "Kensington Addison Road" until 19th December 1946, the day on which London Transport's District Line service to the station recommenced after the war. Another post-war change was the growth in summer holiday trains. Class H2 no. 32422 is working the 2.20pm Hastings to Birmingham train on 1st August 1953 and has passed under Middle Box, which closed in 1958. (J.J.Smith)

105. The south-east bay was the departure point for the 5.6pm to Clapham Junction on 14th June 1954, which required five coaches, the outer pairs being articulated Eurostar style. Note the wooden signal post and the lack of conductor rails. Class H no. 31550 is in charge. (J.H.Aston)

106. Conductor rails for LT and LMS trains were provided on all through lines and at the north-east bay. LT operated a shuttle service from Earls Court during the period of Olympia exhibitions only. The train recorded on 6th October 1954 had hand operated sliding doors. (T.Wright)

107. Ex-SR class W 2-6-4T no. 31925 is running from Hither Green to Old Oak Common in about 1955 as the platform edge is repainted. Few trains used any of the other platforms at that time. A vast quantity of parcels was handled here, much of it emanating from the nearby catering business of J.Lyons & Co. (Lens of Sutton)

108. Class H2 no. 32424 runs towards the down through line with the 12.35pm Leicester (London Road) to Hastings train on 18th August 1956. North Main box closed in October 1982. The remains of the original station buildings were demolished in 1958. (J.J.Smith)

109. Rail mounted road tankers, of a type similar to those reinvented in 1997 for the proposed new West Country milk trains, run through from East Croydon to Wood Lane on the same day. The conductor rails were removed from the through lines earlier in 1956 and from the through platform roads after the south-west bay had been brought into use for LT trains on 3rd March 1958. The locomotive is H class no. 31261. (S.C.Nash)

110. The 11.05am Walsall to Hastings passes through on 11th July 1959, hauled by "Schools" class no. 30900 *Eton*. The north-west bays are being upgraded and provided with a canopy to protect the parcels and their handlers. (J.N.Faulkner)

111. During the rebuilding work at Euston in 1964 some trains were diverted to Kensington Olympia. Class 40 diesel no. D332 arrives with the 8.00am from Blackpool on 20th June as a Pannier tank shunts milk tankers. (J.N.Faulkner)

112. Class 20 diesel no. D8000 arrives on 20th June 1964 with milk tanks to be unloaded in the bay platforms. Note the end loading facility for vans at the north-east bays. (J.N.Faulkner)

113. A group of horse boxes are in the background as 0-6-0PT no. 4609 speeds through on 18th July 1964 with a special meat train. Beyond the bridge is the point where the West London Railway ended and the West London Extension Railway began. (E.Wilmshurst)

114. Resignalling and track alterations at Paddington in 1967 saw most West of England and Worcester line services using Kensington Olympia. No.D1022 *Western Sentinel* has arrived with the 07.55 from Penzance on 18th November while passengers off the District Line shuttle from Kensington High Street hurry towards the 15.20 departure for Worcester. Thirty years later the station still had the best kept waiting room and most spacious toilets in the area. (J.N.Faulkner)

115. No. 59104 *Yeoman Challenger* roars through with empty stone wagons on 2nd December 1990, while an LT train is at the sole remaining bay platform. The signal box closed in October 1992, since which time the area has been controlled from the Victoria Signalling Centre. The IC sign, with its useful information, was soon removed; the new sign indicates that the station had recently become the responsibility of NSE. (A.Dasi-Sutton)

116. Conductor rails were relaid in 1993 for Eurostar trains. The "Kenny Belle" was electrically operated from 26th July 1993 until 27th May 1994 by units such as class 421 (4CIG) no. 1305, seen working the 18.05 on 24th August 1993. Former 4COR vehicles were diesel powered for a period around 1970. (C.Wilson)

117. The impressive Eurostars regularly graced the scene, albeit empty, from November 1994. No. 78 proceeds to North Pole Depot on 13th January 1995. Note that the station had undergone another change of management. (C.Wilson)

118. Class 117 DMUs based at Bletchley maintained the service from May 1994 until November 1996 when electric working recommenced using dual voltage class 313 units. Overhead wiring had been extended south of Willesden Junction to overlap the conductor rails to North Pole Depot. No. L 705 is seen on 19th October 1995 along with historic stock in the little used siding to

the former up platform. The "Royal Statesmen" coaches were often used on luxury railtours and were on show in connection with a travel exhibition in Olympia. (C.Wilson)

119. A new four coach up platform was opened in May 1994, the old one still being visible behind it. Passing through on 1st June 1996 is an HST working a Eurostar feeder service from Manchester Piccadilly, due at Waterloo at 11.46. A similar train from Edinburgh was due at 13.48. Both were withdrawn on 31st May 1997 due to very light loadings and privatisation bureaucracy prohibiting their use by non-Eurostar passengers. The ramps on the down platform lead to portable buildings that can be used by customs officers in the event of a Eurostar train having to use this station in an emergency. They can also be used for the detention of illegal immigrants arriving on North of London Eurostars. (P.G.Barnes)

3

120. The London-Penzance "Night Riviera" was diverted from Paddington to Waterloo in May 1995, to give direct connections with Eurostar. The train was recorded returning empty to Old Oak Common on 3rd October 1997, having left Waterloo at 07.45 in gloomy weather. It is headed by no. 47816, no. 47813 being at the rear and nearest the camera. Next to it is a van and the single sleeping car from Plymouth. The route had become even busier in June 1997 with the addition of hourly weekday trains to and from Rugby, the best Midlands service ever at this station. (V.Mitchell)

121. The launch of the West London Railway album took place in the fine booking hall of Kensington Olympia station on 26th October 1996. This was the 100th volume from Vic Mitchell and Keith Smith and North London Railways presented them both with a full size nameplate to commemorate the event.

MP Middleton Press

Easebourne Lane, Midhurst, West Sussex. GU29 9AZ Tel: 01730 813169 Fax:01730 812601

... WRITE OR PHONE FOR OUR LATEST LIST ...

BRANCH LINES
Branch Line to Allhallows
Branch Lines to Alton
Branch Lines around Ascot
Branch Line to Ashburton
Branch Lines around Bodmin
Branch Line to Bude
Branch Lines around Canterbury
Branch Line to Cheddar
Branch Lines to East Grinstead
Branch Lines to Effingham Junction
Branch Line to Fairford
Branch Line to Hawkhurst
Branch Line to Hayling
Branch Lines to Horsham
Branch Line to Ilfracombe
Branch Lines to Longmoor
Branch Line to Lyme Regis
Branch Line to Lynton
Branch Lines around Midhurst
Branch Line to Minehead
Branch Lines to Newport (IOW)
Branch Line to Padstow
Branch Lines around Plymouth
Branch Lines around Portmadoc 1923-46
Branch Lines around Porthmadog 1954-94
Branch Lines to Seaton & Sidmouth
Branch Line to Selsey
Branch Lines around Sheerness
Branch Line to Southwold
Branch Line to Swanage
Branch Line to Tenterden
Branch Lines to Torrington
Branch Line to Upwell
Branch Lines around Wimborne
Branch Lines around Wisbech

SOUTH COAST RAILWAYS
Ashford to Dover
Brighton to Eastbourne
Chichester to Portsmouth
Dover to Ramsgate
Portsmouth to Southampton
Ryde to Ventnor
Worthing to Chichester

SOUTHERN MAIN LINES
Bromley South to Rochester
Charing Cross to Orpington
Crawley to Littlehampton
Dartford to Sittingbourne
East Croydon to Three Bridges
Epsom to Horsham
Exeter to Barnstaple
Exeter to Tavistock
Faversham to Dover
Haywards Heath to Seaford
London Bridge to East Croydon
Orpington to Tonbridge
Sittingbourne to Ramsgate
Swanley to Ashford
Tavistock to Plymouth
Victoria to East Croydon
Waterloo to Windsor

Waterloo to Woking
Woking to Portsmouth
Woking to Southampton
Yeovil to Exeter

COUNTRY RAILWAY ROUTES
Bath to Evercreech Junction
Bournemouth to Evercreech Jn.
Burnham to Evercreech Junction
Croydon to East Grinstead
East Kent Light Railway
Fareham to Salisbury
Frome to Bristol
Guildford to Redhill
Porthmadog to Blaenau
Reading to Basingstoke
Reading to Guildford
Redhill to Ashford
Salisbury to Westbury
Strood to Paddock Wood
Taunton to Barnstaple
Westbury to Bath
Woking to Alton
Yeovil to Dorchester

GREAT RAILWAY ERAS
Ashford from Steam to Eurostar
Clapham Junction - 50 years of change
Festiniog in the Fifties
Festiniog in the Sixties

LONDON SUBURBAN RAILWAYS
Caterham and Tattenham Corner
Clapham Jn. to Beckenham Jn.
Crystal Palace and Catford Loop
East London Line
Finsbury Park to Alexandra Palace
Holborn Viaduct to Lewisham
Kingston and Hounslow Loops
Lines around Wimbledon
London Bridge to Addiscombe
Mitcham Junction Lines
North London Line
South London Line
West Croydon to Epsom
West London Line
Willesden Junction to Richmond
Wimbledon to Epsom

STEAM PHOTOGRAPHERS
O.J.Morris's Southern Railways 1919-59

STEAMING THROUGH
Steaming through Cornwall
Steaming through East Sussex
Steaming through the Isle of Wight
Steaming through Kent
Steaming through West Hants
Steaming through West Sussex

TRAMWAY CLASSICS
Aldgate & Stepney Tramways
Barnet & Finchley Tramways
Bath Tramways

Bournemouth & Poole Tramways
Brighton's Tramways
Bristol's Tramways
Camberwell & W.Norwood Tramwa
Croydon's Tramways
Clapham & Streatham Tramways
Dover's Tramways
East Ham & West Ham Tramways
Eltham & Woolwich Tramways
Embankment & Waterloo Tramway
Enfield & Wood Green Tramways
Exeter & Taunton Tramways
Gosport & Horndean Tramways
Greenwich & Dartford Tramways
Hampstead & Highgate Tramways
Hastings Tramways
Holborn & Finsbury Tramways
Ilford & Barking Tramways
Kingston & Wimbledon Tramways
Lewisham & Catford Tramways
Liverpool Tramways 1. Eastern Ro
Maidstone & Chatham Tramways
North Kent Tramways
Portsmouth's Tramways
Reading Tramways
Seaton & Eastbourne Tramways
Southampton Tramways
Southend-on-sea Tramways
Southwark & Deptford Tramways
Stamford Hill Tramways
Thanet's Tramways
Victoria & Lambeth Tramways
Walthamstow & Leyton Tramways
Wandsworth & Battersea Tramways

TROLLEYBUS CLASSICS
Croydon's Trolleybuses
Hastings Trolleybuses
Maidstone Trolleybuses
Reading Trolleybuses
Woolwich & Dartford Trolleybuses

WATERWAY ALBUMS
Kent and East Sussex Waterways
London's Lost Route to the Sea
London to Portsmouth Waterway
Surrey Waterways

MILITARY BOOKS
Battle over Sussex 1940
Blitz over Sussex 1941-42
Bombers over Sussex 1943-45
Bognor at War
Military Defence of West Sussex
Secret Sussex Resistance

OTHER BOOKS
Brickmaking in Sussex
Garraway Father & Son
Index to all Stations
London Chatham & Dover Railwa

SOUTHERN RAILWAY VIDEO
War on the Line